CHI

P9-CME-867

MORE ANIMAL HEROES

MORE ANIMAL HEROES

Karleen Bradford

Cover by
Bernard Leduc

SCHOLASTIC INC.
New York Toronto London Auckland Sydney

No part of this publication may be reproduced in whole or in part, or stored in a retrieval system, or transmitted in any form or by any means, electronic, mechanical, photocopying, recording, or otherwise, without written permission of the publisher. For information regarding permission, write to Scholastic Canada, Ltd., 123 Newkirk Road, Richmond Hill L4C 3G5, Ontario, Canada.

ISBN 0-590-18797-X

Copyright © 1996 by Karleen Bradford.
All rights reserved.
Published by Scholastic Inc., 555 Broadway, New York, NY 10012,
by arrangement with Scholastic Canada, Ltd.

SCHOLASTIC and associated logos are trademarks
and/or registered trademarks of Scholastic Inc.

12 11 10 9 8 7 6 5 4 3 2 1   8 9/9 0 1 2 3/0

Printed in the U.S.A.   40
First Scholastic printing, January 1998

Contents

*For the family pets who were
with us for only a short time:
Blackie, Mauricio and Kitty Kat.*

Acknowledgements

I would like to thank all the owners of these wonderful animals for the time they so graciously gave to me and their patience in answering my questions. I would also like to thank Julia McKinnell, producer of CBC's *Basic Black*, who put me in touch with Philip Gonzalez, the owner of the incredible Ginny. Mike Mackintosh, Head of Wildlife Services for the City of Vancouver, and Graham C. Ford, Assistant Manager of the Stanley Park Zoological Gardens, were very helpful with the story of Tuk, the polar bear, whom I was lucky to meet personally — although not *too* personally.

My morning dog-walking friend, Tom Corat, owner of two Great (in every sense of the word) Bouviers, put me onto the story of Max. My good friend Marilyn Lister, a Bernese Mountain dog owner and enthusiast, found the account of Balloo and Jessie for me. Katharine Paterson, another friend who went on the animal hero alert for me, and who has written about search-and-rescue dogs herself, told me about Jiggs.

Special thanks to George Hickinbottom, who has helped me on both animal hero books now. He supplied me with information about Ricky, the pet who went to war.

I was delighted to hear the story of Patsy, the kindly cat, from Sonja Seiler herself, a student in one of my writing workshops.

Finally, I would like to thank Ralston Purina and Lee Ramage of National Public Relations (NPR) Limited for the immense amount of help and information they provided me. I have now been to two of their award ceremonies and loved every minute of them.

Karleen Bradford

Photo courtesy Ralston Purina

Sam and Phyllis

SAM

The Dog Who Remembered

Phyllis McLeod called her dog, Sam, to go out. They usually walked along the edges of a golf course. The Credit River runs through the course, and that year, when the river froze, ice floes had formed. Chunks of ice had pushed up out of the river onto the golf course and gouged their way across the fairways. Then, heavy snowfalls had blanketed the whole area, and the river was buried, running somewhere underneath it all.

"I wonder where that river is flowing today,"

Phyllis said to Sam as they started out. The water was having to find a new path every day under the snow because of the ice build-up.

Phyllis couldn't see any trace of where the river might be. It was a beautiful day, even if it was cold. The sun was bouncing off the snow like diamonds. It was such a gorgeous morning, Phyllis let Sam off the leash to run free. Then, all of a sudden, she felt the ground beneath her give way. The river had found Phyllis — and she was falling into it.

The water was freezing cold, and the current was fast. Phyllis grabbed at an ice floe in front of her, but she could feel her whole body being pulled under. She couldn't put her feet on the bottom — the current was far too strong. Phyllis hung on with every bit of her strength. She knew that if she let go she would be dragged under the ice, and no one would find her until spring.

It seemed to Phyllis that she clung there for an eternity, but it was probably only a few seconds until Sam came back. She stood on the snowy bank above Phyllis. The dog started whimpering and whining, and then pulled at Phyllis's hat. Phyllis tried to reach for her, but

Sam was too high up. She yelled, "Down, girl!" and Sam went down on her belly.

Sam was wearing a choke collar. Phyllis's only chance was to grab for it, but the dog was still almost out of reach.

What if I miss? Phyllis thought, but she was slipping further and further under the ice. There was no other way. With one hand still clinging to the ice floe, she lunged forward and up, grabbing for Sam.

Her fingers closed around the metal collar.

"Pull, girl!" Phyllis shouted.

Sam stood back upon her four legs, braced herself, and pulled. She pulled Phyllis right out of the water and up onto the ice.

"I just hugged her, and lay there, trying to get my breath," Phyllis recalls. "Then I had to walk back home — a good half-hour away. I was afraid I might fall into the river again, because, except for the spot where I fell in, I still didn't know where it was running."

Phyllis put Sam back on the leash and let her lead the way.

"She kind of picked her way around, and I just followed her. I think she somehow could sense where the river was." Phyllis arrived home nearly frozen — but she made it, thanks to Sam.

How did Sam know what "Pull!" meant? To answer that question, Phyllis had to remember back to when Sam was a puppy.

"We've always had dogs, but never a German Shepherd," Phyllis says, "and I had always dreamed of having one. So, for my son Ian's twenty-first birthday, my other two sons and I went shopping and bought this puppy. She was so small, she could fit into the palm of my hand. We all just fell in love with her."

Ian was at university at the time — actually, he didn't really want a dog! — so Sam became Phyllis's dog. She wanted to call the dog Baby or Princess, but the rest of her family laughed at her. "You can't go out at night and call, 'Here, Baby! Here, Baby!'" they said. Phyllis's husband started calling the dog Sam, and soon so did the rest of the family. When they went to register her at the vet's, they were told Sam was a male name. They registered her as Lady Samantha, but she's always been just Sam at home.

Sam was an amazing pup and easy to train, Phyllis says. She was very intelligent and a "wonderful, wonderful pet," although she grew very quickly into a huge dog. When anyone came to the front door, she just assumed that they were there to visit her, and she would wiggle and make all kinds of welcoming noises.

Not everyone appreciated the welcome, especially those who didn't particularly like dogs. In fact, Phyllis's sons found it downright annoying sometimes.

"When they were teenagers and tried to sneak in late at night," Phyllis laughs, "she'd greet them at the door, and the noise of her tail banging against the stair railing would wake up the whole family. I always knew exactly what time they came in."

The only thing Sam was afraid of was thunderstorms. She ran out of the yard once during a particularly bad one, onto the four-lane highway that runs near the McLeod home. A driver thought he had hit her when she ran right in front of him, so he jammed on his brakes and jumped out to see if she was all right. Sam took the opportunity to leap into his car for safety from the storm and wouldn't get out. He ended up taking her to the pound, where Phyllis found her.

Sam was great with children. If someone came over with a baby, she would lie down beside him or her, and if the baby cried, Sam would go over to the mother and pull on her clothes, as if to say, "Hey! Your baby's crying!" Sam loved to play, and it is when recalling Sam's favourite games that Phyllis thinks of something.

"When she was a pup, she had this big rubber dog bone with a ring at one end that a person could hang onto. My sons would play with her with it. She would grab onto it — and you know how a Shepherd's jaws lock — and they would say 'Pull, girl, pull.' She'd tug and hang onto it so hard they could swing her right off her feet. That was when she was a pup, though. Sam was seven years old when she rescued me, but she must have remembered somehow."

Sadly, Sam died in the summer of 1994, just months after receiving the Ralston Purina Award for her bravery.

"She had a beautiful, gentle nature," Phyllis

says. "There was a very strong bond between Sam and me. She seemed to sense my moods. If I was down, she'd just be there for me. She was a character. A wonderful character."

Photo courtesy Toni Emslie

Jiggs

A Champion in Every Way

It was a cold mid-winter day when the telephone rang at Toni and Lorry Emslie's Kadesh Kennels near Kemptville, Ontario. A four-year-old boy was lost. He'd been missing for five hours, and the weather was stormy. The roads were so bad the Ontario Provincial Police and their tracking dogs hadn't been able to get through. Could Toni and Jiggs help? Toni didn't have to think twice. Of course they could.

Jiggs was a Bouvier des Flandres, a big, rugged dog of a kind originally bred in Europe for herding cattle and general farming tasks. He was a champion in conformation (how well a dog conforms to the physical standards of its breed), obedience and tracking. With the help of a professional trainer, Toni had trained Jiggs as a civil guard dog, with a specialty in search and rescue. Jiggs had learned to search in any kind of terrain and weather; to go through or around any obstacle. He could even sniff out people trapped in collapsed buildings. It took around two and a half years for Jiggs to complete this rigorous training, including a year in the United States for a special course in tracking.

Jiggs started young. When he was not much more than a pup, a German Shepherd escaped from Toni's kennel through a hole in the chain-link fence. Toni decided to see what Jiggs could do. She took him over to the fence and said: "Find him." The next thing she knew, she was flying down the road at the end of Jiggs' nine-metre lead. They crossed three fields, then saw the German Shepherd. The dog plunged into a swamp, and Toni couldn't follow. Every day after that, for three weeks, Jiggs went out on his own looking for the dog, until finally the

Shepherd turned up one morning at the back door. "Jiggs lay down with a satisfied air," Toni says, "as if to say, 'Well, I've done it. He came back.'"

Another day, a Doberman named Jet escaped from the kennel. He tore the leash out of Toni's hand and ran away. Jiggs was outside.

"Jet was a male, and of course Jiggs was a male, too, so there could have been problems," Toni says. But Jiggs is a good, peace-loving dog, and Toni knew he wouldn't start a fight. She said: "Go get him!" First, Jiggs ran down to the back of the orchard near the pasture, where the Doberman was heading, and just stood there. Jet swung away from him, heading for the woods. Again, Jiggs ran ahead and blocked the way. "Everywhere that dog went, Jiggs was there before him," says Toni. Finally, Jiggs herded Jet back up the driveway. Toni quickly opened the door of the car and called, "Come on, Jet, let's go for a ride!" The Doberman fell for it and hurled himself into the car.

With such good herding skills, Jiggs' one weakness was not surprising: he liked to chase sheep. "There's something that happens to a dog when it smells a sheep, I think," says Toni. "I had a little lamb that grew up to be a very stupid ewe. She would follow me everywhere, but if she ever started running, I would see an ugly gleam come into Jiggs' eyes. He never took off after her, but he certainly did slobber and drool a lot." Toni laughs. "I think he firmly believed that stupid sheep *should* be chased!"

Jiggs played with Toni's little daughter all the time, but if visitors drove in, he was immediately between them and her until Toni came out and said it was okay.

"If I was ever stiff or unwelcoming, Jiggs made it clear that he wouldn't tolerate the visitor either. It made people pretty uncomfortable when he just stood and stared at them," Toni says. "He was a very large dog."

Despite his size, Jiggs was so well behaved that Toni could take him anywhere. "All of Kemptville knew him," she says. "He was allowed in every store in the town. Everybody loved him. I would go into the bank and say 'Stay,' and he would lie there as long as I wanted him to. One time, a little girl came and sat beside him and started to read him stories. A man came up and greeted her mother, then reached down to ruffle the girl's hair. Jiggs gave him a good growl. 'He won't bite,' I said. 'He's just looking after the child until her mother's done.' He was like that. Very protective."

Jiggs' protectiveness and his calm way with children would be needed, one stormy winter day.

When the call came in, Toni had a moment's doubt. For all Jiggs' training, he had never actually tracked a real person yet. The conditions were so terrible, and the child had been gone so long already — would Jiggs be able to find him? She knew she had to let him try.

The boy had been with a group of children and adults tobogganing on a hill near the woods. Somehow or other, he had wandered off.

"We had a little piece of the boy's clothing," Toni says, "and I gave it to Jiggs to sniff. Then we took him to where they had been tobogganing. Now this is the incredible thing," she goes on. "In the intense cold, the scent does not hold for long, and there were so many tracks around there. I thought, well, this time I can't follow him around on a lead. I've got to let him free. That dog searched and that dog searched, and I had to keep on stopping him to get the snowballs out of his paws. He would not quit. All of a sudden, right near the edge of the woods, he took off and bounded through the trees."

Toni clambered through the bush after him, but then she lost him.

"I thought, *I'm* going to be lost now," Toni says. "I kept on yelling, 'Jiggs, speak!' the whole time. He would give the odd woof — enough for me to keep track of him."

Toni trailed the dog for an hour and a half. When she finally found him, he was sitting in the middle of tangled undergrowth, with vines wrapped all around him and the little boy hanging onto his neck, snuggled up to him for warmth. Jiggs wouldn't leave the boy, even to come to Toni.

The other searchers caught up to them. Then it took another hour to carry the boy through the deep snow and back out of the woods. The boy's mother was hysterical with relief, but the little boy himself was calm and cheerful. He was much more impressed with "the big dog that came and found me."

"He hadn't really realized the danger he was in," Toni says. "When I found him he just asked, 'Where's Mommy?' I told him she was back with the others, and asked him why he had gone off.

" 'I followed the bird,' he said. 'It was a pretty bird.' "

Jiggs died in 1989. The whole community mourned him. In an obituary printed in the *Kemptville Advance* on the anniversary of his death, he was described as "a champion in the conformation ring, obedience ring and in the tracking field but above all, he was a supreme champion at heart. He gave of himself to the minute he died. He would tackle any task put before him without question and put his life on the line for anyone in his family."

Photo courtesy Philip Gonzalez

Ginny

A Cat's Best Friend

Philip Gonzalez suffered an industrial accident that left him partially disabled, and he was depressed.

"You need a dog," his friend told him, so they went to the animal shelter near Philip's home in Long Beach, New York. The man at the shelter worried that perhaps Philip wouldn't be able to take care of a dog, so he suggested a cat.

"I don't want a cat," Philip answered. "I want a dog. A big dog."

The shelter officer showed him the dogs they

had there, but none seemed right to Philip.

"I've got a couple more in the back," the man said, so they went to have a look.

The first dog Philip saw was a female Doberman Pinscher.

"I don't want a female," he said.

Then he saw a young Schnauzer/Husky mix. When the dog saw Philip, she got up, came over to him and started licking his hand.

"That's a first," the shelter officer said. "We haven't been able to get this dog to respond to us at all."

"I'll take him," Philip said.

"It's a her," was the answer.

"Well, then, I don't want her. Besides, she's too small."

"Take her around the block," the officer insisted. Philip's friend urged the same. So Philip gave in. Halfway around the block, he looked down at the dog following him. She looked back up at him, and that was it. Ginny was his. He took her back to the shelter and told them he was taking the dog.

On the way out, Ginny stopped at one of the cages and sniffed at it. There was a black puppy in it. Ginny started to lick the puppy. "That's her pup," the officer explained. "She's only about a year old, but she had three puppies when we found her abandoned in the closet of an empty house. The others have found homes — I'm sure this one will, too." And it did.

But Ginny's maternal instinct just grew stronger. The first day Philip took her for a walk where he lived, they came across a cat. Ginny pulled on her leash, and Philip, still not too strong after his accident, dropped it. She ran toward the cat, and he was afraid she was going to attack. Far from it.

"She and that cat starting kissing each other, and then they played for almost an hour," says Philip.

Ginny loved every cat she saw, and soon Philip was feeding the strays around his house. He took Ginny back to the animal shelter for a visit, and she headed straight for the cat cages. She put her paws up on one and started whimpering.

"She looked back at me, and I knew she was asking me to get that kitten for her, so I said, 'Okay, Ginny, I'll take the cat,'" Philip says. "I figured she liked playing with the stray cats so much, she wanted one of her own."

Philip brought the little white kitten home and named her Madam. About two days later, he found out she couldn't hear a thing, but neither he nor Ginny minded that.

On another visit to the shelter a couple of weeks later, Ginny picked out another cat: Revlon, who had only one eye. Then Philip took Ginny to the veterinarian's for a checkup. There, she spotted a cat that the vet was going to put down. It had no hind feet, and it was very wild. Ginny made it clear that she wanted it.

"Ginny, this cat's wild," Philip told her, but she wouldn't listen. So Betty Boop went home with Philip and Ginny, and she got on just fine.

The next two months brought two more cats, Topsy and Vogue. On a walk, Ginny got off the leash again and ran into an abandoned building. She came out carrying a kitten in her mouth. It seemed hurt, so Philip took it to the vet, who found that it was brain-damaged.

"You want me to put it down, right?" the vet asked.

Philip looked at Ginny, who was watching them anxiously.

"No," he answered, "I don't think Ginny would like that."

So Topsy joined the growing family.

Ginny rescued Vogue from some people who were kicking her in the street. At first, Philip thought the tiny creature was a kitten too, like Topsy, but the vet said she was eight or ten years old. Once she started eating, she grew into a very big cat.

One rescue followed another, and before long, Philip had nine cats — quite a number for someone who hadn't wanted even one. But Ginny wasn't through saving cats. Not by a long shot. The place where Philip lives is a resort area. People come for the summer, bringing their cats, and when they go home in the fall, they leave their cats behind. Life is hard for the cats, and they have to fight for survival. Ginny helps whenever she can.

"The cats on the street trust Ginny more than they trust me," Philip says. "People around here can be mean to cats and throw rocks at them. They're really leery of humans, but every cat in the neighbourhood trusts Ginny."

Ginny doesn't put up with human bullies, letting them know with a good growl just what she thinks of them. But she'll protect any cat at all. King Arthur is a big Russian Blue cat, grey with white patches. He was a street bully, but then the other cats got together and ganged up on him. He fled to Ginny, and she protected him. Philip brought him home, and, under Ginny's watchful eye, he behaves beautifully.

Other animals are wary of Ginny, too. One of the cats in Philip's household, Dotty, used to live in a junkyard. "There were a bunch of chickens running loose in the yard that used to beat up Dotty all the time. About eight of them, that used to attack her," remembers Philip. "Ginny went over there and stopped that. Those chickens ran when they saw her. Then she found this really big tiger-striped cat there too, with a hurt leg." Both Dotty and Napoleon, the tiger-stripe, went home with Ginny and Philip.

Because of Ginny, Philip has a reputation for being a cat's best friend as well. One day, someone called Philip and told him they had a female pure-bred Manx cat named Sheba, but they couldn't keep her. Could he take her? Silly question. Philip picked her up and took her to the vet to have her spayed. There, he found out that Sheba was really a male, so there was a quick name change: Sheba became King Solomon.

These days, Philip feeds about ten cats on his terrace and goes on rounds twice a day to eight different spots, where he and Ginny take care of another sixty to seventy cats. At one of the feeding spots, Ginny ran over to an abandoned car. "She started whimpering and trying to get into it, so I went over," says Philip. "When I got there, I saw this cat lying there, but it had been dead for at least a couple of days. I told Ginny, 'Look, there's nothing I can do. The cat's dead. I'll pick it up later and take it to the shelter.' But she kept whimpering at me and wouldn't leave. I went back, and a kitten put its head up from behind the big cat's body." A closer look revealed another kitten. The two were about two weeks old. It was the first really cold night that winter, and without Ginny's help, the kittens would have been dead by morning. The kittens were very cute, all black with white bibs and feet —

"tuxedo kittens," Philip calls them. They were soon adopted.

Ginny is almost six years old now. "Some months go by and she doesn't find a thing, other months, she just keeps on finding cats," Philip says. She's found over two hundred by now. "And I've never had one die," he adds.

Ginny made the front page of their community newspaper, and they did a two-page article on her. She's also had an entire book written about her by Philip himself and Leonore Fleischer. It's called *The Dog Who Rescues Cats, The True Story of Ginny*.

The Heroic Polar Bear

Tuk is an old bear, about thirty-four years old. He has lived far longer than any polar bear would in the wild, and almost the longest of any polar bear in captivity. He spends most of his time lying in the sun sleeping, nose twitching at the occasional fly. Looking at him, you would never imagine that years ago, when he was a young bear, he saved a life.

He was brought as a cub to the Stanley Park Zoo in Vancouver in 1961, along with three other polar bear cubs. A special Polar Bear Grotto was built just for them at the zoo, and they settled in. It was the best Polar Bear Grotto the zoo could build at that time. Mike Mackintosh, the head of Wildlife Services for the City of Vancouver, came to work at the zoo as a student volunteer when the bears were about five years old, and he's been there ever since. He got to know them very well. There were two other males besides Tuk, Old Man and Grump, and a female, Lady.

When the bears were young, they used to play together. They were in and out of the pool all the time, running around, diving in, tumbling all over, and shoving each other. When they slept, they would lie together in one big ball in the central den.

"But they all had their own unique personalities," Mike says. Grump was the biggest, weighing nearly 500 kilograms, but Old Man was the boss. Old Man was bothered for much of his life by arthritis, and was quite a bit slower than the others, but there was no doubt that he was in charge.

Grump was Mike Mackintosh's personal favourite. "He was all roar and no action," Mike says. "He was a very active bear and in outstanding physical condition. He could stand and touch his nose to the top of the Bear Grotto, which was almost four metres high. Kids watching him would just gasp in awe. We'd toss fish to him, and when he stood and put his feet up against the sides to support himself while catching them, it was incredible how much space those feet would cover."

"As big as dinner plates," Graham Ford, the assistant manager at the zoo, describes Grump's feet.

"He was a very, very interesting bear," Mike says. "I was really fond of him."

Lady was the most predatory of the group. "Of all the bears, I considered her the most untrustworthy," Mike says. "I used to think that in spite of the fact that she was the smallest of the bears, if any one of them was going to eat me, it would be her." She was quite aggressive. When she wanted something, she didn't hesitate to tell the others off, even Old Man.

Mike describes Tuk as the "serendipity bonzo" of the group, a bit of a prankster and rather a free spirit by polar bear standards. "One

Photo courtesy Karleen Bradford

Tuk

of his favourite jokes was to lunge at people coming into the feeding den. Standing quietly off to one side, he would wait until someone had walked up close to the bars. Then he'd suddenly leap forward, rather like a dog might." Mike and his co-workers played along. They would bring visitors, especially kids, in to watch the bears feeding, and smile as Tuk made them gasp and jump away.

"He still does it," Graham says. "Even though he's old. I call them play charges." It may be play, but the keepers are glad there are bars between them and the bear. "We sometimes pat him through the bars, but you have to be careful," Graham continues. "You never know when you're going to lose a finger. Polar bears can't be trained. You'll never see one in a circus. They're more ferocious than other bears." Tuk has lived in a zoo nearly all his life, but he is not tame. He is not a pet.

One sunny summer day, there was the usual crowd of people, mostly children, around the Bear Grotto. The bears had just been let out for the morning, after being fed. Tuk was lying on the parapet overhanging their big pool. He was sprawled out on his stomach, dozing lazily in the sun. Suddenly two young men came running by. As they ran past, one of them reached underneath his jacket, pulled something out, and threw it into the pool. To the horror of everybody around, a young kitten hit the water with a splash and sank below the surface. Everyone screamed.

Tuk woke up. He opened one eye and looked over the edge of the pool. The kitten was just a small blob under water. Tuk stood up and stretched, and the people around the grotto held their breath. Did the little kitten look like dessert to the massive bear? Tuk yawned, then he slid into the water. Children screamed again. A few seconds later, Tuk surfaced. The tiny cat was pinned delicately between Tuk's front teeth by the nape of its neck, just the way a mother cat would carry her kitten. Tuk swam to the edge of the pool and hauled himself out, dripping water. Still holding the kitten carefully in his teeth, he lumbered back up onto the parapet. Then he lay down. He flattened the kitten with his enormous paws, opened his huge mouth — and began to lick the tiny creature dry.

The other bears were beginning to take notice, and they didn't look as friendly as Tuk. The zookeepers frantically tried to get the bears separated. It took well over an hour, but finally they got all except Tuk inside. It took a while longer to convince Tuk to leave the kitten and go inside the pen as well, but at last they succeeded. The little kitten was fetched out of the grotto and taken home by one of the volunteer workers.

Tuk is still living at the Stanley Park Zoo. He's the last one left of the four bears. Polar bears are by nature very solitary animals, and Tuk doesn't seem to mind being alone. In fact, he seems happier without Lady bossing him around. The zoo is going to be closed soon, and the other animals relocated, but not Tuk. He's too old to be moved someplace new. So, the grotto will stay as long as Tuk lives. In the meantime, he has "the best we can give him," Mike Mackintosh says. The best medical care and the best food. Chicken, fish, horsemeat, whole salmon, animal meals, oils, vitamins, carrots, beef, herring, minerals and bones — Tuk eats everything.

"He has as good a life as we can afford him," Mike says. "And he deserves it."

The Pet Who Went to War

Dogs have gone to war since the days of the Egyptian Pharaohs thousands of years ago. Even before that, they guarded the caves of Stone Age people and hunted with them. Packs of ferocious hounds accompanied the Persians when they conquered Egypt in 526 B.C. War dogs, wearing spiked collars and chain mail, fought beside the soldiers of Rome. Right up to modern times, dogs have had their part to play in the wars that people fought. Mostly, these dogs were big and fierce, trained to kill.

ond World War, however, a new
dog came into being. The British
ely needed guard dogs. They also
ng dogs to help the soldiers move
safely into enemy territory, dogs to carry
messages, and ambulance dogs to pull carts and
stretchers. They needed thousands of dogs, in
fact, and they didn't have them. So they
appealed to the people of Britain to lend their
pets.

The people responded, and dogs begin to
arrive at military headquarters all over the
country. Among them was Ricky, a Welsh
Sheepdog, who belonged to Mr. and Mrs.
Litchfield of Bromley. Ricky was sent to serve
with the mine-detecting platoon of the British
army.

Dogs were very valuable to mine detectors.
They had found that a dog was usually too light
in weight to trigger off a mine. Dogs, along with
their handlers, could be sent ahead of advancing
troops to sniff out the mines safely. The platoon
was soon training dogs by the hundreds.
Gradually, it began to look like a dog show
around there. No animals were ever treated

better, and the dogs were in top condition. T
were intensely enthusiastic about their work.

Ricky took to the change from pampered pet
to army dog immediately. He was trained using
the reward system — a biscuit for him every time
he sniffed out a buried mine — and was soon
collecting his share of the treats.

In 1944, Ricky was landed in Europe as War Dog
6883, attached to the Royal Engineers, and kept
by Sergeant Yelding of the Royal Army
Veterinary Corps. Now he was working for real,
helping to clear mines off roads and railway
tracks while the battle went on around him. On
December 3 of that year, he was working in
Nederwent, Holland, clearing the edges of a
canal bank. One by one, he found all the mines.

Then one exploded. The section commander
nearest to Ricky fell, injured by the blast. Ricky
himself was bleeding from a wound in the head.
But Ricky kept right on working. Without the
least bit of fuss, ignoring the blood, he found a
path through the mines. Through that path the

Photo courtesy G. Hickinbottom

Ricky

section commander was brought to safety. Then, he and Ricky both received medical treatment.

Ricky received the Dickin Medal of England. It was inscribed "For Gallantry, We Also Serve." The Royal Society for the Prevention of Cruelty to Animals awarded him the "For Valour" medal and a certificate, on which was written: "For outstanding ability, courage and devotion to duty while on active service with the British Landing Armies, from D-Day to the cessation of hostilities during the World War, 1939-45."

Ricky did such good work during the war and established such a good reputation for himself that, after the war, the War Office offered to buy him from his owners. Mr. and Mrs. Litchfield did not accept the offer, though. They were too glad to have him back home, safe and sound after all his adventures.

Photo courtesy Ralston Purina

Balloo and Jessie with Ursula

Berners to the Rescue

Wanda Tait and her daughter, Ursula, flew to Holland to pick up a Bernese Mountain dog named Brigitte. Some years later, Brigitte had her last litter of puppies. Because Brigitte was very special to them, the Taits decided to keep one of these puppies. That was Balloo.

"His personality made itself known very early on in life," Wanda says. "He was always very laid back and independent. The other puppies would all be playing or eating or whatever together, and he would be off doing his own thing — chasing a butterfly, maybe. He was an independent thinker from day one, but he was also a cuddly puppy. He was actually the first dog we ever let sleep on the bed with us. He wasn't so big at first," Wanda says, "but Berners *grow*. Now, when my husband Eric comes to bed, he has a hard time finding a place for himself!"

Balloo is a champion show dog, but he also knows how to work. Bernese Mountain dogs were originally a Swiss multi-purpose farmer's dog. In particular, they were drovers, dogs who help move cows. They were also used to pull carts. In the summer the farmers would take the sheep and the cows up into the mountains to pasture. The Berners pulled carts with big metal cans full of cream down to the cheese-makers in the valleys. Then they hauled the empty carts back up into the meadows again. Balloo lives up to the tradition by pulling carts and sleds for the Tait family.

"He's our tow rope — like a ski lift," Wanda says. "The girls toboggan down the hill and he pulls the toboggan back up. It's very nice to have him there, because we have a great big, long wooden toboggan that seats six. Everyone loves riding down the hill on it, but it's awful to pull back up. The snow sticks to it. Poor old Balloo gets the job. He doesn't mind at all, though. He's just happy to be there. He takes the girls and the kids in the neighbourhood sledding, too," she adds. "They hitch him up and go for rides all around the place."

The Taits kept one of Balloo's first puppies, too — Jessie. Jessie is a happy dog. She's large for a female, almost as big as Balloo.

"We call her the couch potato," Wanda says. "She doesn't like to be hot, so when she's on the family-room sofa, she stretches out the whole length of it, from end to end, on her back with her tummy up. No one else can sit there."

The Taits live in Rocky Mountain House, Alberta, and love hiking. A friend of theirs made backpacks for the dogs, so whenever they go camping or for picnics, Jessie and Balloo carry their own food as well as some of the family's supplies. In wintertime, when the family goes cross-country skiing, the dogs carry extra gloves and socks.

Whatever the season and whatever the activity, the dogs are pretty useful to have along.

But the Taits didn't know how far their usefulness could go until one frightening day.

Fifteen-year-old Ursula Tait was a member of a Search and Rescue program organized by the Royal Canadian Mounted Police. The program teaches basic first aid, and there are also courses in white-water rescue, rope climbing and ice climbing. Ursula and her best friend Nina Hofer had been part of it for over a year and had been on quite a few search-and-rescue missions. On one of them, they found an animal trail that led along a steep hill to a beautiful, wild sort of place. They wanted to go back to it, and when they did, a few weeks later, they took Balloo and Jessie with them.

"As we walked up the trail," Ursula says, "I had a headache. I had taken some Tylenol, and I got dizzy. I don't know exactly what happened, but I fell."

Ursula plunged about fifty metres down the hillside. To Nina's horror, she was headed straight for rocks and a tree. Balloo lunged after her. He got beneath her and used his body to stop her fall.

Nina worked her way down the hill to Ursula as quickly as she could, with Jessie following. Ursula was unconscious. She was bleeding from cuts on her head, back and legs. When she regained consciousness, after about five minutes, she was able to talk to Nina, saying her back hurt. Both girls knew the dangers of moving a person with a back injury, so they decided Ursula had better stay as still as possible and they would wait for a rescue party to find them.

"We weren't scared," Ursula says. With all their rescue and survival training, the girls knew just what to do. Nina built a fire and covered Ursula with extra clothes and blankets from their backpacks. Balloo had not moved from where he had thrown himself to stop Ursula's fall. Now, both dogs curled up as close to the injured girl as possible, Balloo at her side and Jessie at her head.

The temperature dropped to three degrees Celsius that night. "The dogs kept me warm the most," Ursula says, "I mean, the whole night we were shivering, but without the dogs, it would have been a lot worse. It rained off and on and it was really cold." Nina had to keep moving Jessie, who was tucked in so close to Ursula's face that the girl could hardly breathe.

The two girls heard coyotes or wolves howling all through the long hours of darkness, but they knew the dogs would keep off any animals that came prowling during the night. (In fact, the next day they did find fresh bear tracks around their campsite.) Early the next morning, just at the break of dawn, Ursula and Nina heard a rescue team calling out to each other on their radios. They heard someone say that they could see a fire. The girls knew it must be theirs.

Nina blew long and hard on her whistle and then yelled. A yell came back. Within minutes, one of the searchers came running up the hill.

"The dogs went wild," Ursula says, "but they were so protective — at first, Jessie wouldn't let anyone near me."

The area was too isolated and the bush too dense to get an ambulance in, so a helicopter flew Ursula out, immobilized on a flatboard. Luckily, she was only in the hospital for a day, and there was no serious injury to her back.

Balloo and Jessie were both inducted into the Ralston Purina Hall of Fame in 1996 for their heroic actions. Only Balloo was able to go, however, as Jessie was expecting pups. He flew to Toronto with the Taits to receive the awards. And he revelled in all the attention that came with them.

Photo courtesy Vera Soudek

Dolly and Max with Vera

MAX

The Protector

Max the Bouvier and Dolly the Dachshund are the best of friends. Sometimes they get into trouble, and it's usually Dolly who gets them into it. But Max is the one who gets them out.

Dachshunds are hunters. They were originally trained to burrow into the dens of badgers and foxes. Once underground, they could not hear commands, so they had to be able to make their own decisions. Independent thinking was the character trait a dachshund's master prized most, and that trait has survived in the breed to this day.

When Vera Soudek got Dolly, the dog was so tiny Vera could hold her in one hand. She was a sweet little dog, but 100 percent dachshund.

"For example," Vera says, "I would say 'Down.' Dolly would sit and then look at me as if to say, 'This is good enough, isn't it?' Or when I said, 'Give me a paw,' she would roll over, then later on she would suddenly come over and give me her paw, all on her own. But she's very brave, and not scared of anything."

When Dolly was a year old, Vera got Max. Vera had always wanted a Bouvier des Flandres. Bouviers are *very* big dogs, however: as a puppy, Max was already as big as Dolly. So Vera was a little concerned. But she needn't have worried. When Max saw Dolly for the first time in the backyard, he yelped and ran away. Dolly had never seen a dog like Max, but she wasn't the least bit scared. In fact, she decided to become his mother. While Max was young, if any other dog attacked him, she defended him — even though she was smaller than he was!

Now that he is full-grown, *Max* has become

the family protector. Vera remembers one day when she took him out in the car. It was a hot day, and the window was down. Max was lying on the floor of the front seat, out of sight of anyone outside the car. Vera stopped at a red light. Suddenly, she saw a hand reach through the window of the passenger side and pull up the lock button. Max sat up, and his great head rose into view. The hand disappeared as quickly as it had appeared. Vera never even had time to glimpse the person it was attached to.

And, one day, Max came to the rescue when Dolly's instinct for hunting got her into trouble.

That day, Vera decided to take the two dogs for a walk on Bell's Island, on the Cataraqui River. "It's a beautiful place," Vera says, "full of big old trees." And it was a lovely, early November day. There had been a few cold nights already, and there was a thin layer of ice on the river. It was sunny, and the trees were golden. There was no one else around, so Vera let the dogs run loose. They ran ahead of her, out of sight, and she was just about to whistle them back, when suddenly a volley of barking broke out. Mixed in with the barking was another sound — a strange noise Vera couldn't identify.

Vera started to go after the dogs, then realized that the ground was becoming very marshy. Carefully, she made her way by stepping from one clump of vegetation to another. Meanwhile, the barking and the other strange noise were getting more and more ferocious. Finally, she came to where Dolly and Max were, at the river's edge. There was a terrible commotion going on in the water. Vera saw that the dogs were fighting a raccoon. Dolly's hunting instinct had led her to tackle something much too fierce, even for her.

As Vera watched in horror, the raccoon grabbed Dolly by the ear and dove under the water, dragging Dolly down. Vera knew that this was a raccoon's favourite way of fighting, as it can stay underwater much longer than a dog can.

"I didn't know what to do," Vera recalls. The water was deep, and the bottom was covered with thick mud. The river current was strong, too, and there was a good chance Vera would get swept in if she tried to wade in and help. But, if the raccoon held Dolly down much longer, the little dog would drown.

The rear end of the raccoon was still above water. Max saw his chance and took it. He locked his jaws around the raccoon's back and shook. Finally, the raccoon let Dolly go. She surfaced, covered in mud, with blood streaming down her ears. It had been enough for her. She splashed out of the water and streaked for the car, parked about two kilometres away.

"I hated to leave Max," Vera said, "but I thought, he's a big strong dog, he can handle a raccoon. So I went after Dolly."

Max followed her in a very short time.

"I don't know whether he killed the raccoon or not," Vera says. "It seemed to be tired out. I think it probably just gave up and ran away." But not before biting Max viciously on the legs.

Vera took both dogs to the veterinarian. Dolly's ears healed up nicely, but Max's legs got badly infected. His front legs were so badly injured that, for a while, they were afraid he would never walk again. He did heal, but he was bandaged for weeks. "He was a good patient," Vera says.

Dolly and Max have their breakfast together every morning now. Dolly likes to be wrapped in her blanket and then cuddle back into bed with Vera. Max rather likes being in the bed, too, but he gets too warm and has to get down onto the tiles to cool off. They're still the best of friends, and so far, since their fearful raccoon encounter, they've managed to stay out of trouble.

PATSY

The Kindly Cat

"This short-haired brown tabby with orange colouring is about nine months old. She is very friendly and would make an ideal pet." That's how the ad for "This Week's Pet" ran in the newspaper. The Seiler family was looking for a friendly cat, and they'd been told that calicoes and tabbies were the friendliest, so they decided to go have a look.

What they had heard was true. Of all the cats at the Smith's Falls animal shelter, the young tabby definitely had the friendliest face, four-year-old Sonja decided. The family took the

Photo courtesy Renata Seiler

Patsy and Daisy

cat home with them and named her Patsy (although Sonja immediately nicknamed her Pumpkin Face because of her orange colouring). The Seilers never did find out where Patsy had come from, but her thick, heavy fur hinted that she was an outdoor cat.

Everything was new to the young cat in the Seiler home, and at first she was a bit scared. Perhaps it was the first time she'd ever been part of a family. But Sonja and her younger sister, Monika, loved and cared for her, and it wasn't long until Patsy settled in.

"She really loved being rubbed on her stomach and would purr and purr," Sonja says. When the sisters tried dressing her up in doll clothes, however, she wouldn't stand for it. Patsy was much too dignified for that! She was independent and very good at catching mice. But she was also very affectionate.

Six years after Patsy came, Daisy joined the family. Daisy was one of a litter of kittens born on the farm next door. She was a calico cat — another friendly one. Patsy adopted and loved Daisy right from the start. Good mouser that she was, she kept the kitten well supplied with mice.

Daisy didn't mind being dressed up in doll clothes. Sonja calls her a Gumby cat because she'll let herself be twisted into almost any shape, just like the bendable character of that name. In the winter, she'll curl around the girls' necks like a scarf — Sonja can even wear her like a belt. But Daisy wasn't a placid kitten. From the start, she was very good at climbing trees and getting up in the girls' tree fort. "She loves climbing," Sonja says. "She walks on the smallest branches. She's like a daredevil. She does flips up there."

Sonja and Monika's father, Dieter, is allergic to cats, so he built houses in the garage for Patsy and Daisy. The two boxes are insulated and heated with a battery warmer. The garage itself has lots of beams for cats to climb and jump off. One of Daisy's favourite tricks is leaping onto the sloping windshield of their van and sliding down it. Dieter Seiler also constructed a solar house on the front patio for the cats. It is a wooden box with one slanted, Plexiglas side. When the sun is out, it's as warm as toast in there.

No matter how cozy, the cats sprang from the solar house when Sonja and Monika came outside, especially in the morning when the girls walked up the road to meet the school bus. The cats waited with the girls until the bus came, and often came tearing up the driveway to greet them when they got off the bus in the afternoon.

One morning in early spring, when she was still a kitten, Daisy decided she was tired from the walk to the school-bus stop. She curled up just where she was and fell asleep, the way that kittens do. Patsy was off in the bushes, exploring, and Sonja and Monika were talking as they waited. The bus loomed over the rise in the country road, and the girls got ready. Then they noticed Daisy, sleeping peacefully — right in the path of the bus.

"Daisy, Daisy!" Sonja screamed. But the kitten just slept on.

Out of the bushes streaked Patsy. With a rush, she charged at the kitten, dashing almost under the wheels of the bus, and chased it out of the road to safety!

Patsy is gone now, and Daisy is a full-grown cat. A new kitten has come to the Seiler house.

Perhaps Daisy will care for that little kitten as well as Patsy cared for her.

Photo courtesy Ralston Purina

Bruno and Donnie

A Boy's Best Friend

It was a hot sunny day in August. The Skiffington family was enjoying the weather at their cabin in Lethbridge, on the eastern coast of Newfoundland. The cabin is on a bay, and so close to the water the family can watch whales swim past.

Eleven-year-old Donnie wanted to go swimming, but his parents were busy and there was no one to go with him. He decided to go for a bike ride instead. Of course his dog, Bruno, went with him. Bruno is the family's German

Shepherd and Donnie's best friend and protector. Donnie and his brother Jeffrey had given Bruno to their mother, Cindy, for Christmas, and from the very first he was a playful and loyal pet. He quickly became the boys' guardian. When he was only eight months old, a moose came into the garden where the boys were playing, and Bruno chased it out. "Chased it out of the garden and clear across the road," Cindy Skiffington says.

Bruno is best friends with the family cat as well. Cindy was a little worried about how he would react when the little kitten arrived. But he took to her right away. "It was just a little kitten, but a feisty one," Cindy says. "She took to Bruno, too, and they play together and sleep together. Sometimes Bruno leans down and sort of paws at her to get her attention. Then, when he's asleep, she'll go over and nip on his ear. Some nights we'll see them asleep, and he'll have his two huge paws wrapped around her. He's so huge, and she's so tiny. He'll take her right in his mouth, but he'd never nip her, and she's never had any fear of him. They even eat out of the same dish.

"Some people think dogs are stunned," Cindy

goes on. "They think they're just dumb animals, but they're not." She gives an example of just how understanding a dog can be. One winter, when they were in the woods trying to get a really heavy log out, Eric, Donnie's father, turned to the dog.

"Bruno, grab hold of the rope now and give me a hand, hauling this log," he said. He didn't really think the dog would do it, but Bruno trotted right up, grabbed the rope in his teeth and pulled. Together, they got the log out.

On this particular day in August, Donnie decided to bike over to see a friend who lived nearby. On the way was a steep hill, and Donnie went down it fast. The grass was still wet and slippery from the morning mist, and when he tried to brake, the bike skidded and struck a rock. Donnie was thrown off. The bike hit him in the face, then Donnie careered on down the hill. Catapulted into a ditch at the bottom, he was knocked unconscious. He lay still, bleeding.

Bruno raced back up the hill to get help. He

found Cindy first, but when he bounced and barked at her, she just thought he wanted to play.

"Goon," she said, "I haven't got time for you today."

Then Bruno went on over to Eric, who was up on the hill sawing wood. Eric didn't pay any attention to him either, so Bruno bolted back to Donnie. He grabbed the collar of Donnie's shirt, and began to drag him out of the ditch and back up to the cabin.

At this point, Donnie began to regain consciousness.

All he can remember now is something wet and slobbery pulling him along. He started to cry. Eric and Cindy heard him crying, and ran to help. When they reached him, they could see that Donnie's face was covered with blood. There was a big gash on his forehead, and his eye seemed to be bleeding as well. Luckily for Donnie, although he had to have sixteen stitches in his forehead and four in his eyelid, his sight was not affected at all.

Friends who stayed at the cabin while the Skiffingtons were at the hospital said that

Bruno never left the doorstep. He just sat there, watching and waiting for Donnie's return. When he finally heard the van, he got excited. He rushed to meet Donnie, then followed him as Donnie's parents helped him back into the house and onto the couch. Bruno stationed himself beside the couch, and wouldn't move as long as Donnie was there. In all the days following, while Donnie recovered, Bruno refused to leave his side.

Bruno was given the Ralston Purina Award. He and the Skiffington family were picked up at the airport in a special limousine, and they were given two days they won't ever forget. Bruno had his own doggy sitter while the Skiffingtons toured Toronto.

On the way home, there was a mixup in the flight schedules, and Bruno ended up waiting for the rest of the family at the St. John's airport for several hours. It didn't bother him a bit. In fact, he seemed to enjoy all the attention he got from people coming up to his cage, where he lay waiting.

"They talked to him and gave him water," Cindy says. When the family finally caught up to him, he was having a great time. "He's a wonderful dog." That's what the Skiffingtons say, and they mean it.

WRINKLES

The Brave Little Dachshund

On their way home from Florida, Floyd and Lila Lockyer stopped overnight at a motel. Early the next morning, they were packing up the car to leave. Floyd went back into the room to get the last bags, telling Lila she could bring Wrinkles, their nine-year-old Dachshund, out to the car. As he went to close the motel-room door, two men started to push their way in. Alarmed, Floyd tried to shut the door on them, but one of them stuck his foot in the opening and then forced his way in. He had a gun. Lila turned around and saw him, and as she did, the intruder pointed the gun at her and Wrinkles.

Wrinkles hadn't been feeling too perky that morning and he was still lying on the bed, but as soon as he saw the intruder, he leaped up. He jumped off the bed and attacked the man. Small as he was, Wrinkles got him by the leg and didn't let go. The man pointed the gun down at Wrinkles and fired. Luckily, the shot missed. At the same time, Lila rushed forward to help Wrinkles, but tripped and hit her head on the door frame.

With Wrinkles hanging on to his ankle in determination, the gunman decided he'd had enough. Trying to shake the dog off his leg, he backed up and out the door. Floyd managed to pull Wrinkles off and slam the door shut.

"The second guy was right behind the first one," Floyd says. "He didn't get a chance to do anything because the first one backed up when Wrinkles got hold of him. Without the dog, there was no way we could have protected ourselves."

Lila was bleeding quite badly from a gash on her forehead. Floyd called 9-1-1, and help was there almost immediately. After spending several hours in the hospital, Lila was released, and the family was able to go on home the next day.

Floyd and Lila got Wrinkles when he was a four-month-old pup.

"He's very protective of us," Floyd says. "Dachshunds are protective little fellows. But he's a very loving dog. If I'm in the living room, sitting in a chair, he wants to get up on my knee. He's certainly our hero and a good companion."

As the Lockyers found out after they got home, the reason Wrinkles hadn't been feeling well that morning was that he had developed diabetes. The veterinarian told them that they could either treat him or put him down.

"We thought, how could we put a dog down that had just saved our lives?" Floyd recalls, so they started treatment. The dog had to go into the animal hospital for a while until they got him on insulin and got the diabetes under control. Wrinkles is home now, and Lila gives him an insulin shot in the morning and at night.

Unfortunately, because of the disease and his age — he's twelve years old — he has become blind. But he still gets around fine.

"He's got his favourite little places in the house where he lies," Floyd says. "He can get around real well." He gets a little shaky sometimes, and a bit disoriented, but he still goes out for walks when the Lockyers go back to Florida.

"He likes that," Floyd says. "You have to be his guide dog when you go out for a walk. But he's spunky. When somebody comes to the door, he sure lets us know they're there."

Wrinkles received the Ralston Purina Award for his bravery. Part of the award was a supply of dog food, which he couldn't eat because he is on a special diet. So the Lockyers donated it to an animal shelter where they live.

Photo courtesy Ralston Purina

Wrinkles with Lila and Floyd

Photo courtesy Ralston Purina

Lindy with David and Margaret

Who Made a Lucky Choice

It was a crisp November afternoon when David Downie set out for a walk with his dog, Lindy. He got only about seven metres away from his home when he suddenly suffered an attack of angina and fell, unconscious, into the snow.

Lindy, leash trailing, set out for help. She ran past several townhouses in the neighbourhood, then came across a man and woman in a car, backing out of a driveway. Lindy started to run back and forth behind the car, not letting them move. The woman in the car got out and picked up Lindy's leash, intending to get her out of the way. Immediately, Lindy began to pull her toward the spot where David Downie lay.

By the way the dog was acting, the woman realized something was wrong. She let the dog lead her and found David. By this time, David was vomiting blood. But the woman didn't panic. She knew just what to do. She turned David onto his side so that he wouldn't choke, then told her husband to call 9-1-1. She covered David up with a sleeping bag to protect him from the cold. It was fortunate for David that Lindy had picked the perfect person to help her master: Eleanor Craig, who just happened to be a registered nurse.

In the meantime, a neighbour passing by recognized Lindy. He took her home and alerted David's wife. David came back to consciousness briefly as they loaded him into the ambulance. The next thing he remembers is waking up in the hospital with his wife at his side.

"We like to joke about the clever choice Lindy made in finding a registered nurse to help me," David Downie says now. "But we know that Lindy's very special and we'll be forever grateful to her."

David and his wife, Margaret, got Lindy when she was about a year old. Some people who wanted to get rid of their dog put an ad in the newspaper, and David and Margaret saw it. When they went to look at her, Lindy was outside, tied to a stake on the lawn. David asked if he could take the dog out for a walk. The people told him she'd never been for a walk.

"She was over a year old, and she'd never even been for a walk!" David says with disgust. "She'd obviously been abused. She would cower every time you so much as looked at her." He and Margaret felt sorry for the dog and took her home with them. They set about the task of teaching her to trust people again. Luckily for David, Lindy learned.

Lindy never did learn to be obedient, though. "She's a Border Collie/Basset Hound mix, and that's the Basset Hound characteristic," David explains. "If you called her, she'd go the other way. She'd go around in a big circle, and eventually come, but her own way, and in her own time. We went to Basset Hound trials once, and even there they wandered all over the place. So we didn't feel so badly because Lindy wasn't obedient."

Lindy loved David and Margaret's grandchildren. They used to come over, and she liked nothing better than playing with them.

Lindy was awarded the Ralston Purina Animal Hall of Fame Medal. Sadly, at the same time she developed cancer. David and Margaret left her with their family veterinarian while they went to Toronto to accept the award for her. Ralston gave them a beautiful painting of Lindy, so they have that to remember her by, and her picture was in the *Winnipeg Sun*, looking as happy and bright as ever, even though it was taken while she was sick.

"She never complained, all through her illness. She was a good dog," David says.

And a dog who more than repaid the kindness that David and Margaret showed to her.

Trained to Track

Constable Tom MacLean had never worked with police dogs before, but he'd always had dogs of his own, so he applied for the Canine Team program. He was accepted and assigned a two-and-a-half-year-old, long-haired German Shepherd named Ewo, a dog with "a sort of a wolf look to him." The two began a training course with the Niagara Regional Police Force. Thirteen weeks later, they both graduated with flying colours.

Ewo's specialty is tracking, mostly on a

nine-metre lead. Off lead, he is trained to bark when he finds what he is looking for — usually a person — to let Constable MacLean know where he is. Ewo has also learned to jump hurdles and fences, go through tunnels, climb ladders, walk across catwalks, and search for and retrieve objects. He's normally a friendly dog, but is trained to be aggressive when necessary. He will protect Constable MacLean or anybody else, and will chase and apprehend a criminal — by biting and holding the suspect's arm.

Good dogs for the police force are hard to find: only about one in 300 dogs makes a successful police dog. It might seem surprising that one of the most important things the police look for in a dog is a friendly, sociable nature. This is because, as Constable MacLean says, "you can train a dog to be aggressive, but it's hard to calm a wild one down."

Potential police dogs should have a good retrieval instinct, too. They have to love to chase balls, for example. They can't be afraid of loud noises, traffic, stairs, doorways, slippery floors. They must be confident and brave — but willing to accept their trainer as the boss.

It's a long list of requirements, but Ewo met them all. And training him was easy. "It's harder to train the trainer than the dog, to tell the truth," says Constable MacLean. "Dogs do it naturally."

The key to training a dog is play and a "praise and reward" system. Constable MacLean explains: "When the dog does something good he is rewarded, and we all act goofy and make it fun for him. He remembers, 'Hey, if I do a good job, or do this right, I'm going to get to play.'" The police use a special toy called a Kong, a cone-shaped, bouncy thing that dogs love to chase. The officers hide the Kong, and the dogs learn to track trying to find it. When the Kong is found, the dog gets to play: chasing after the Kong, wrestling with his handler and getting "lots of pats and lots of praise."

All this play makes Ewo great with kids. "Ewo is the kind of dog that you can take into a kindergarten class and the kids can crawl all over him," Constable MacLean says. The two used to visit classrooms to demonstrate a police dog's skills. Kids loved Ewo's specialty,

Photo courtesy Ralston Purina

Ewo and Constable MacLean

something no other dog would do.

"We put him in a baby carriage," Constable MacLean remembers. "We put a bonnet on him, and he would just lie there. Then I put on a dress and a wig. We would walk along, and then somebody would steal my purse. Ewo would jump out of the carriage and go and bite the guy. It made a great show."

But for all his playfulness, Ewo was ready in an instant when it was time for him to go to work for real.

On December 17, 1992, an elderly couple returned to their home near Niagara Falls to find three men robbing their house. The men ran out the back door and disappeared into the bushes. The couple called the police.

Constable MacLean and Ewo arrived on the scene about forty minutes later. They knew the direction the men had gone, and Ewo picked up their scent immediately. Constable MacLean put Ewo on his lead. With an escort officer for safety, the team headed into the bush. After a short while, they came across a garbage bag full of Christmas gifts that had been taken from the house. Further on, they found a coat. Ewo was getting excited.

They kept on, across fields, through thick bush, and across dense cornfields. After about an hour, Constable MacLean suddenly saw one of the thieves running ahead of them in the bush. The man stopped and darted behind a tree. As the dog and trainer approached, he suddenly came out from behind the tree, swinging a big stick. Constable MacLean sent Ewo in to attack. Ewo grabbed the man by the arm, and the escort officer arrested him. But that was only the first robber; there were at least two others.

The team kept on tracking for another hour and forty minutes. They crossed a couple of little creeks, and then a big one. There wasn't a lot of snow on the ground, but it was bitterly cold, and this creek was partly frozen. Constable MacLean could tell by the broken ice that one of the men he was pursuing had waded across, and he decided to go after him. He took off his gunbelt and threw it across the creek to an officer on the other side. He threw his gun across, too. Ewo swam across on his lead, then Constable MacLean plunged into the freezing water. Luckily, it wasn't over his head, but it was up to his armpits and the current was strong. With the help of his fellow officer, who pulled on Ewo's lead, Constable MacLean made it across safely. Then he continued tracking, soaking wet and very cold.

Ewo was performing exceptionally well. Normally, a dog will lose interest after a short period of time — most of the tracks are only a few hundred metres, or at the most a kilometre, but Ewo just went on and on. "After he got the first guy, he wanted number two," the constable remembers. "His interest didn't flag at all."

After about fourteen kilometres, they went into a farmer's field, bordered by bush in which there was an old abandoned car. Ewo went into the bush and started whining and barking, and Constable MacLean found the second thief, dug in under the car. The man was arrested. The third thief got away, but the two who were arrested were confirmed criminals, well known to the police.

Constable MacLean had to go to the hospital

to be treated for hypothermia, but didn't have to stay long. As for Ewo, who had worked so hard and for so long in the below-zero weather, he was so tired they had to lift him into the police car.

Ewo is retired now, and Constable MacLean keeps him as a pet, much to his children's delight. During his career, Ewo did many brave things. One of them stands out in the constable's memory — and still brings Ewo rewards.

On Valentine's Day one year, a seventy-two-year-old woman was walking down the street. She was attacked by a young boy, who knocked her down and stole her purse. The elderly woman had a cut in her head, and she had to crawl to a house to get help. Ewo was called and tracked the boy down successfully. The woman's purse was returned to her intact. Every Valentine's Day since then, the grateful woman sends Ewo a big present: a Valentine's card, dog cookies and bones.

"It makes it all worth it," Constable MacLean says.

Ewo was given the Ralston Purina Police Dog of the Year Award in 1994. He took the stage with Constable MacLean, and let everyone know just how pleased he was about it. As the Ralston Purina spokesman was introducing him, Ewo began to talk. He growled and yowled and barked, and went on growling and yowling and barking — so much that the presenter of the award could not make himself heard.

"Do you want to tell the story yourself?" the presenter finally asked.

It seemed very much as if Ewo did.

Photo courtesy Ralston Purina

Topnotch and Jim

The Faithful Friend

Irene Thomson used to do the accounting for the local feedmill near where she lived in Moffat, Ontario. There is some bush near Moffat that's quite wild, and often she would see hunters' cars parked there. One Saturday morning, arriving as usual with her husband, Jim, they saw a terrified little beagle running around. They coaxed it over to them and gave it something to eat.

The next weekend the dog was still there. They fed it again. The little dog began to trust

85

them. They checked the paper for any notices of a lost beagle, but after another week, they decided that the beagle had been dumped on purpose.

Irene wanted to take it home. Jim didn't really want to, but finally he consented. It was a decision that would save his life.

Topnotch was a good, quiet little dog, and very affectionate. He never ran away, the way so many other beagles do. He didn't seem to have any hunting instinct at all, which was probably why he had been abandoned — someone had tried to make a hunter out of him, then abused and dumped him when they were unsuccessful.

Jim started to take the dog on walks with him, and it wasn't long before the small dog became his constant companion.

One morning, Jim and Topnotch left the house around noon. When evening came and they hadn't come home, Irene got worried. Her husband suffers from Parkinson's disease and Alzheimer's, and she was afraid he might have become confused and lost. She called the police, who immediately started a search.

Five days later, Jim Thomson still had not been found. The area is full of trees and swampy ground — and coyotes.

"That's what we were afraid of," Irene says. "Those coyotes howled all night. I thought for sure they got the dog, at least." The searchers started looking for the dog's remains, hoping that would give them some clue as to where Jim might be.

Every morning, when Lynn McBratney came into the Halton Regional Police Station where she works as a station duty clerk, the first thing she asked was whether there was any news yet about Jim Thomson. The answer was always no. "Finally, I just got a real gut feeling that I needed to do something about it," Lynn says. So she asked Sergeant Kim Duncan, who was coordinating the search, if it would be all right if Lynn got a few friends to come out and help. The sergeant was glad to give permission, so Lynn rounded up four friends and the brother of one of them, who was visiting from the Yukon.

They went out bright and early the next morning, and soon were up to their hips in a swamp.

"It was hot — the hottest day of the summer," Lynn says, "and mosquitoes were everywhere."

About noon, Sergeant Duncan took them back to the command post. Many of the other searchers left at that point, but Lynn and her friends were determined to keep on. An auxiliary sergeant, John Tatham, joined them, and the party was taken out to the Shannon Trail. It had been searched a couple of times before, but the rescue parties were getting desperate.

"We were thrashing here and thrashing there," Lynn says. "I was getting far away from the others and couldn't see them, so we were calling to each other to keep in touch. It was really heavy bush in there."

Suddenly one of Lynn's friends called out, "Is that dog tied up?"

"What dog?" Lynn called back.

They all came back to the trail, and Lynn's friend said, "There's a dog barking there." They all stood staring, trying to see if the stand of bush was the back of a farm. It could be a farm dog they were hearing — or it could be Jim Thomson's dog.

"His name is Topnotch," Lynn said. "Let's call him."

So they started calling his name, and were answered by a volley of excited barks.

"Where is that coming from?" Lynn's friend's brother, Ross, asked.

"There." The friend who had first heard the barking pointed.

"Ross hit the bush like a knife," Lynn says, "and about ten seconds later he yelled, 'He's here!'"

"The dog?" Lynn yelled back.

"No. Mr. Thomson!"

Lynn and the others charged into the bush. One stayed out to mark the spot where they had gone in.

Jim Thomson was unconscious and lying in two or three inches of water. He was covered with mosquitoes and other insects. There beside him, refusing to budge, sat Topnotch.

John Tatham, the auxiliary sergeant, radioed for help. Not five minutes later, Sergeant Kim Duncan came running in, unable to believe they'd actually found the missing man. The other members of the search team were quick to arrive, along with members of the emergency response team. They widened the trail so that the ambulance officers could get in, and Mr. Thomson was carried out on a stretcher.

A police officer led a worried Topnotch on an improvised leash behind his master. The little dog struggled along the path, but a felled tree in his way finally proved too much for him.

"He just sat down as if to say, 'I've run out of energy,'" Lynn says. "So my friend picked him up and carried him the rest of the way out. When we got back to the command post, we gave him some water and some Timbits."

Topnotch had stayed beside his master for five days and nights. If it hadn't been for his barking, Jim Thomson probably would have died before he was found. The little beagle proved to be a faithful friend indeed, and was one of the inductees into the Ralson Purina Animal Hall of Fame in 1996. He took his place proudly beside the other winners, including Balloo from Alberta, whose story is also written up in this book.

FREDDY

The Santa Dog

The Grand Marshal of the Edmonton Santa Claus Parade in 1994 wore a dark grey coat. He was small, with curly hair. His name was Freddy; he was a hero, and he was a dog. He had saved his owner Sylvana Burnette's life in a most unusual way.

Sylvana had come to Canada from England three years before. One of the saddest things she had to do was leave her dog, Rambo, behind, although she left him in a good home with a friend. Once she was settled in Edmonton, she began to look for another dog. She scanned the newspaper ads every day, hoping to find a Yorkshire Terrier puppy to take the place of Rambo. There didn't seem to be any ads for Yorkies, but one day she saw a notice from someone searching for a home for their five-year-old Maltese/Poodle cross.

"It seemed sad that an older dog like that had to leave the home he grew up in, and I wondered why," says Sylvana. She didn't want an older dog, and she wanted a Yorkie, but she called the owner of the dog, just out of curiosity. She found out that the dog's owner had remarried, and the dog and the new husband didn't get along. "After thinking about that poor little thing for a while — if they didn't find a home for him he would go to the pound — I thought, maybe we could just help each other here. I could give him the home he needed, and he could end my yearning for a 'furry friend,'" Sylvana says. She went to see the dog, and Freddy came home with her.

By the second day, he seemed to realize that he was there for good, and he settled right down. Soon, Freddy was Sylvana's shadow, following her everywhere. "He's a very intelligent dog," she says. "You have to spell out words like walk and food." Sylvana laughs. "And he can tell you exactly what he wants all the time. He taught himself to get up on his hind legs and dance around in a circle whenever he wants a treat."

Sylvana and her husband, Allan, take Freddy everywhere. He loves it when they go camping in the summers, and he especially loves the water. One time he got a shock. They were camping on Elk Island and had driven around to see the buffalo that roam free there. Later, when they were going for a walk in the woods, Freddy ran ahead of them up the trail and started barking at something around the bend.

"Suddenly, we felt the ground shaking and a noise like thunder. Back around the bend raced Freddy, and he did a flying leap into my arms. We realized he'd picked on a buffalo! We ran and hid behind a tree until the great big thing went thundering by. It was good for us that the wind was blowing toward us or it would have smelled us. Stupid dog," Sylvana adds, affectionately.

Freddy has all kinds of toys — fluffy bears, balls, and chew sticks — but his favourite possession is a baby blanket. He stuffs it in his mouth when he goes to sleep. It's the only thing he will not let anyone take from him. Sylvana says she has a real job trying to wash it. She has to put Freddy out in the yard and then sneak the blanket into the washing machine.

One summer day in the middle of August, Sylvana was feeling hot and sticky and decided to take a refreshing bath. She poured her favourite peach bath oil into the water, filled the tub to the brim, then lay back to relax. Sylvana has asthma, and sometimes hot baths can trigger an attack. She started wheezing, and knew she should get her medication. She remembers thinking, "Boy, is this bathroom ever getting steamed up!" as she tried to stand. Then, she fainted.

The next thing she remembers is waking up, coughing, still in the bathtub. Freddy was in there, too, jumping all over her. Sylvana pushed him away. "Get off me, you silly dog!" she said. Then she realized there was no water in the tub. She looked over at Freddy and saw he had the bathtub plug in his mouth. Somehow or other, Freddy must have jumped into the tub after Sylvana fainted and pulled out the plug!

"He saved my life," Sylvana says. "I must have gone under the water because my hair was soaking wet, I had a mouthful of bath oil, and there was a bump on the back of my head. I don't know how he did it, but he did. I was stunned."

When the news got around, Freddy made the front page of the local newspaper, complete with photographs. Radio and TV shows in Canada and the United States were on the phone for interviews. Freddy was a star! The culmination of all the attention was the invitation to be the Grand Marshal of the Edmonton Santa Claus Parade. They dressed Freddy up in a Santa Claus suit with reindeer antlers, and he and Sylvana led the parade, sitting in a bright red bathtub.

Freddy is still famous. When Sylvana takes him for walks, people crowd around him. Gifts for him arrive in the mail every day, especially from children. People shower him with treats and food. So much, in fact, that Sylvana has had to put him on a strict diet — he was getting fat.

"I truly believe that Freddy was meant to come into our lives to do the wonderful and heroic thing he did," Sylvana says. "He probably would have gone to the pound if it hadn't been for me, so I guess I saved his life. And in return, he saved mine."

Photo courtesy Sylvana Burnett

Freddy

UGLY SISTER

The Vigilant Cat

The *Ottawa Citizen* reprinted a short article from China's *Sichuan Daily* newspaper. It told of a cat named Ugly Sister, who saved her master, his wife and their five children. She woke them late one night by meowing, scratching, and even pulling on the trouser legs of her owner, alerting them to the fact that the walls of their two-storey mud house were crumbling. The family escaped just minutes before the building collapsed, and no one was hurt.

Perhaps the family changed their cat's name afterward, in gratitude to their rescuer.

Karleen Bradford has lived all over the world, and now makes her home in Ontario. She is the award-winning author of many novels, including *The Haunting at Cliff House*, *The Nine Days Queen* and *There Will Be Wolves*. She has also written a guide for young writers, *Write Now!*

There have always been pets in the Bradford family, and currently Karleen and her husband share a home with their dog, Tiff (pictured here). Karleen once heroically saved Tiff from drowning.